Go Ask A Bear

M.P. Jones, Jr.

ISBN: 9798325709371

DEDICATION

To our furry friends.

ACKNOWLEDGMENTS

Thanks to whoever came up with the stupid
question in the first place?

Go Ask

A Bear

By

M. P. Jones, Jr.

The hypothetical
scenario tearing
people apart on social
media is this simple
question:

Would you rather be alone
in the woods with a man
or a bear?

Not unanimous,
but a good number of
women on TikTok,
Instagram and
YouTube

preferred

the bear.

"Bear! Definitely a bear,"

she said,

"Men are scary."

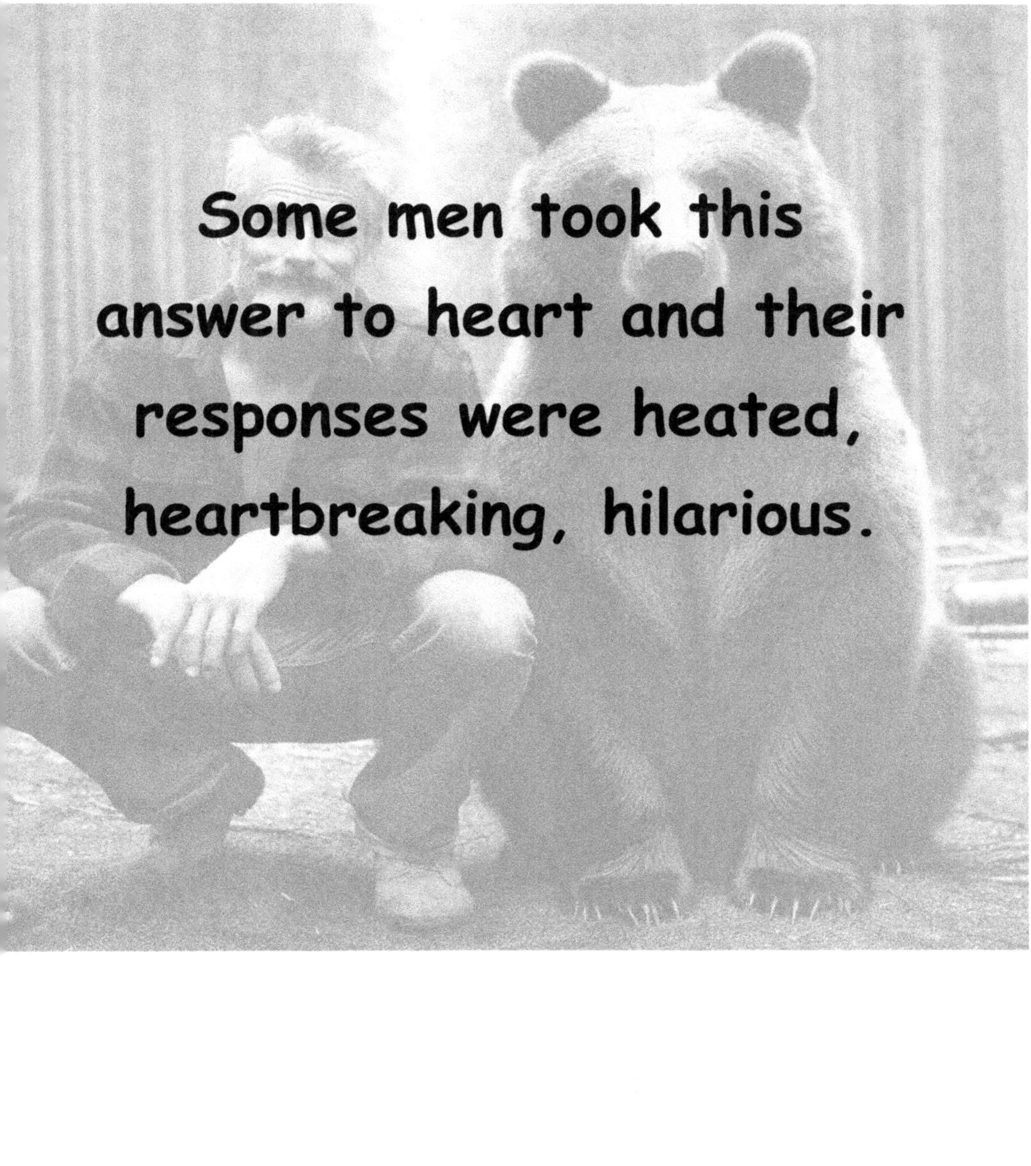

Some men took this answer to heart and their responses were heated, heartbreaking, hilarious.

The audacity to think you could survive a grizzly bear attack!

AVERAGE 343%
AVERAGE 8.5%
AVERGEE 1.5%
ACE 695%

"I bet these women think that the real bears are like their plush Teddy Bear toys."

"So now if I'm on a hike and hear a woman scream for help I'll continue my hike and hope a bear helps."

"Is it wrong to use their logic against them?"

"If you hear a random scream in the woods in the U.S. chances are it's cougar in heat - still safer than a woman these days."

"The bear deserves to survive. The woman affected on the other hand, well she made her own decision and don't need no man to help her."

Bears Lives Matter

"Well, no,

of course, because no woman
who actually leaves her house
and doesn't live on social media
would actually pick the bear.

Never forget that you are getting selection bias, the type of woman who would choose a bear is the type of woman who had never been near the woods IRL. A woman who goes on hikes is going to be vastly different from those simpletons. "

"This is why when my friend and I saw two drunk girls who'd just crashed their car in the middle of the night, said *'Daaaaamn sucks to be them'* and kept on driving."

Go Ask A Bear!

"Dude NO... the bear might choke on a septum ring or get poisoned by hair dye and bad tattoo ink.

"This
whole
stupid
trend is

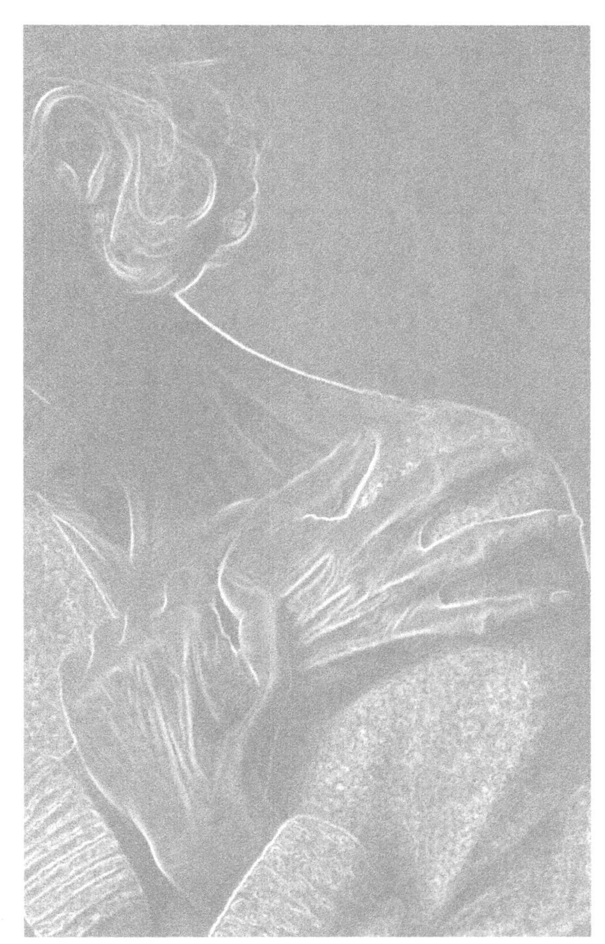

perpetuating "all men are
a threat" type of
misandry.
If men said something
similar, it'd be sexist

and misogynist."

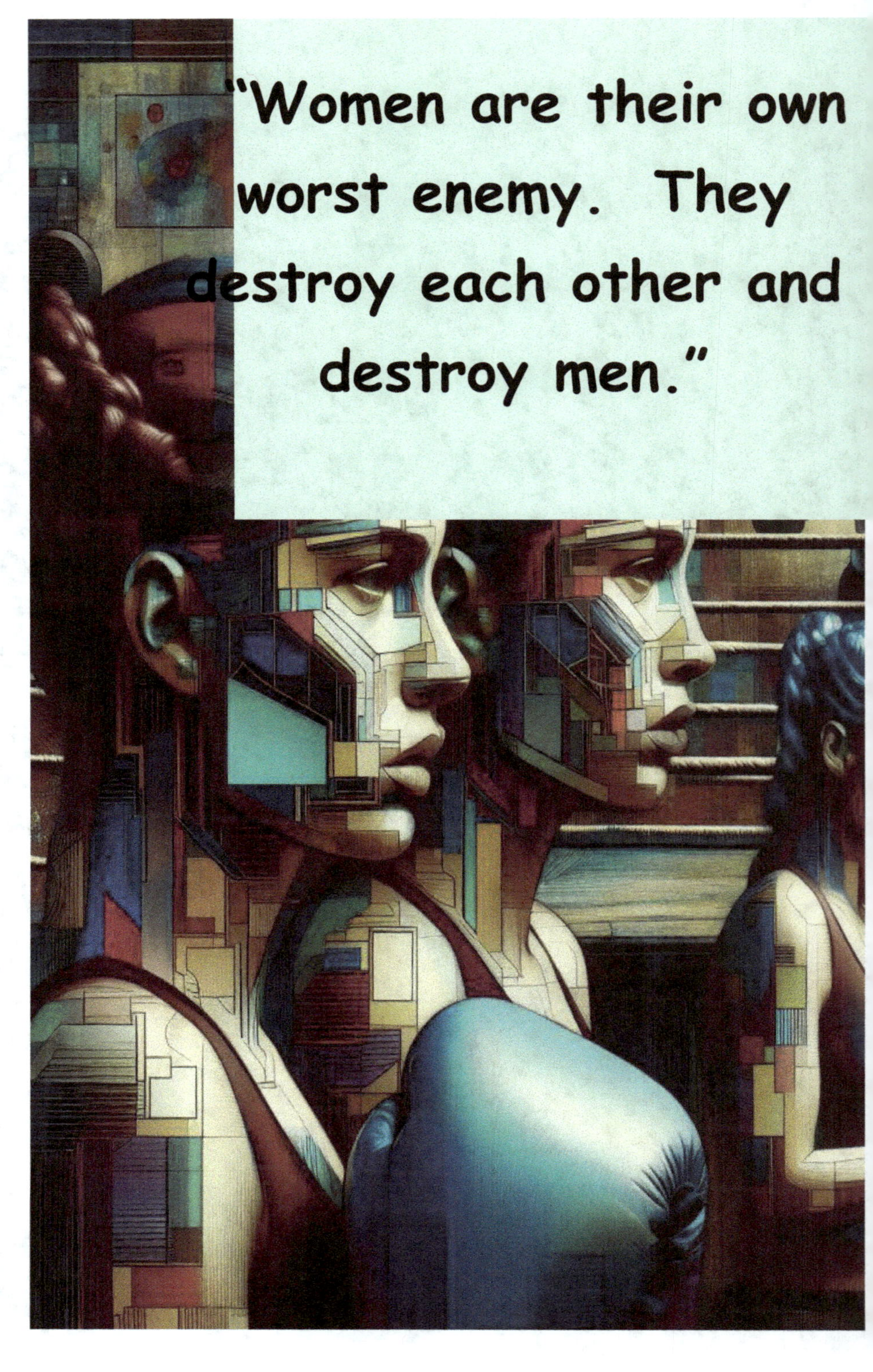
"Women are their own worst enemy. They destroy each other and destroy men."

"I would rather stay up late in office with a bear roaming the halls rather than a woman colleague.

That's because if

the bear attacked me I can get

others to

believe

me.

But if the woman attacked me and claimed assault, I would

spend my entire remaining life
trying to get sympathy for being
falsely accused."

"Women: We're all
team bear.

Bear: so you have
chosen death."

"Their need to antagonize men is so blatantly obvious that it hurts."

The eternal question.
Without an answer.

"Interesting how the wife will immediately think of the men as the most dangerous thing while assume the bear will

be a cuddling

little cub.

Sure is fascinating with indoctrination and stupefied.

"6% of
Americans
think they can
beat a grizzly
bear in a
fight."

"Perhaps the
bear is just a
man wearing a
costume."

"40km per hour top speed women think they can outrun a bear. They can climb trees as well.

You're dead hon. "

"Like a baby black bear, maybe and I mean HARD MAYBE a fully grown man or woman could scare one off, sure I could

believe that but it's still iffy at best.

A hungry adult
grizzly? My son
there are survivor
stories where
people have let
loose 5 or 6 shotgun
blasts to the

bear's face and

it won't back

down.

This is no bird shot
btw, this is either 0-

0 buck or slugs, shit that can easily penetrate the thick body of a bear and shatter bone, and the fucking

bear don't give up."

"They chose the bear, seems only right to respect their wishes."

"If you're in the woods
and see/hear a woman
attacked by a bear,
would you save her or let
her be attacked?"

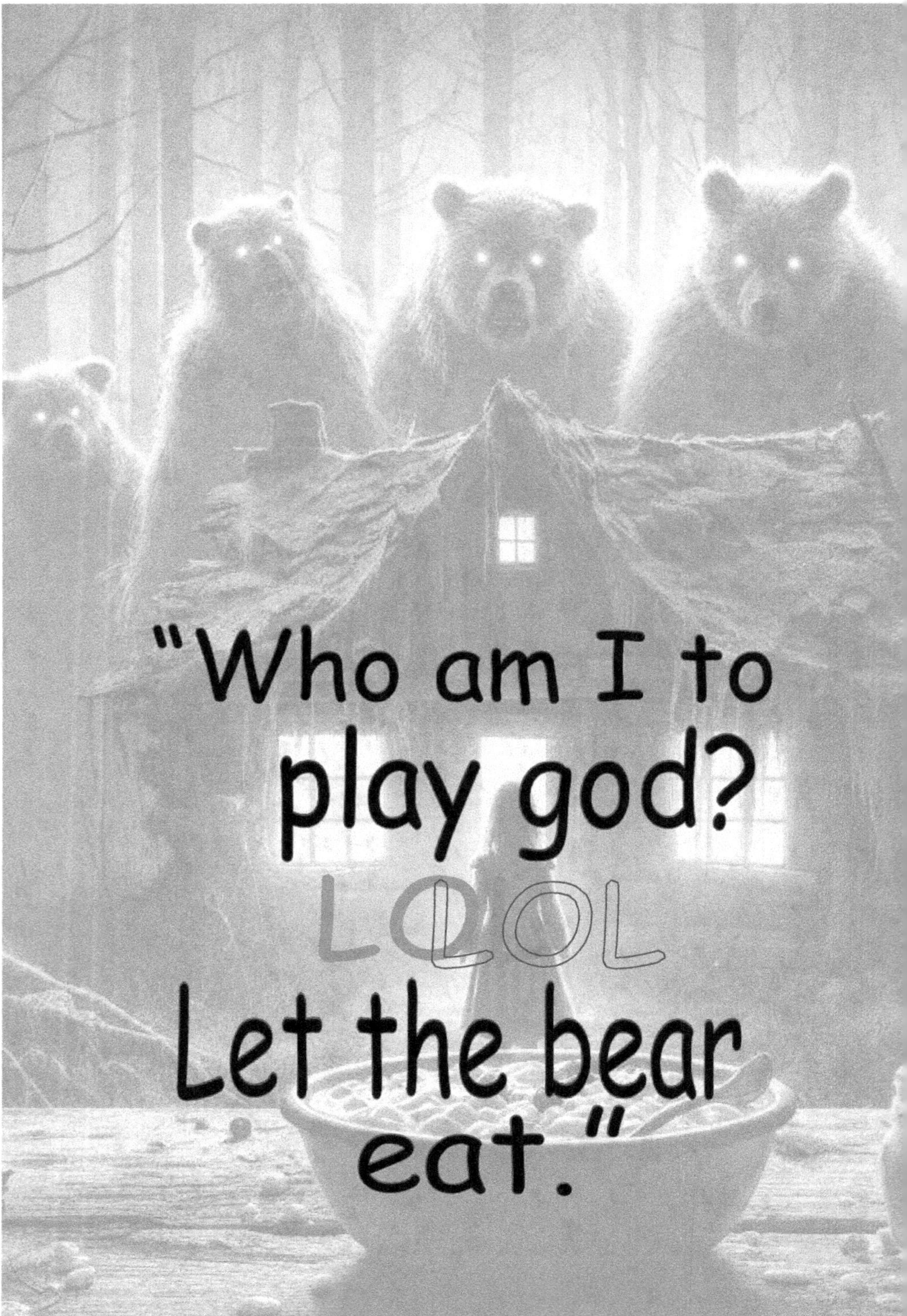

"Who am I to play god?
LOL
Let the bear eat."

"I read a story about a man who helped a woman with her flat tire on a road in a remote place.

The next day he was charged with SA and he lost his job.

I would avoid helping women and especially kids. If a kid needs help or is crying somewhere in public call a woman to help or better just move along. There is no point in risking your entire life for this. "

If a woman is
screaming for
"help"
she's trying to set
someone up.
Ignore and
walk away.

Not worth it.

"Many modern men would just push the woman in front of the bear."

"Of course,
otherwise at the
end the army of
misandrists will
say the bear
saved the woman
from you"

"The craziest
part is... it's still
easier to fight
off a man than a
fucking

BEAR!"

"Wake up call for men."

"Maybe Islam isn't so wrong after all..."

And what are
women saying on
social media
after reading
men's
responses?

"Look, I'm a woman. Comparing a bear to a man is not good because it assumes all men are sexual predators. If you were a man you'd be offended too. The question comes off sexist by saying all men are less trustworthy than a bear.

I believe there was a much better way of making a point about sexual assault without attacking

someone"

"This isn't just about sexual assault. It's trying to show how prevalent threatening situations involving a man are in any women's lives. We've been there enough that our automatic reaction is to pick the bear..."

"It's not assuming all men ae sexual predators, if that were true, we wouldn't love our brothers and our husbands. It's point out how widespread the issue is for women. Widespread enough that we know there is a good likelihood of not being safe in the woods with that random man...."

"For the women who chose the bear, that is not an attack on men.

Men have become so defensive about it, that it's become an argument.

There is no argument needed. A question was asked, bear was chosen and now men need to listen to the WHYs.

Them getting worked
up and offended is
not helping and is
not

women's fault...."

"Listening and understanding the why's would be a much more thoughtful and productive reaction, but here we are,

...

...being invalidated again."

The question
that started out
as a silly "If you
encountered..."
has morphed
into much
more.

...

"Your attitude is defeatist and

Alienating

.

The reason I find this discussion ridiculous is not because I'm a man. I can fundamentally understand the underlying

implications and
the why's...."

The reason I
find this
conversation
ridiculous is
because it's like
talking to a brick
wall that
invalidates my
life experience
solely on the
basis of my
genitals.

WOMEN

"Women know who
to trust and who
NOT to trust.
Bears, like most
wildlife, are afraid of
humans. They don't
discriminate between
men and women. Bears
are never assholes. "

"Sorry you
men are taking
this so
personally.
Evolution favors
survivors and
women are
choosing the
bear to

survive."

And what about the bear?

What does the bear want?

Bears want
to live in
the woods...

Bears want to shit
in the wood...

Bears
don't care
if people
ask each
other
stupid
questions
....

Bears just
want to be
left alone...

Whether you are a man
or a woman walking in
the woods, leave bears
alone and pick up after
yourselves...

It's not up to
bears to solve
human
problems.

So, what has the question

Would you rather be alone
taught us?
in the woods with a man
or a bear?

For one thing, we've learned that social media is a place for international discourse.

A place where

people who
would never
meet face to
face have the
chance to read
opinions vastly
different from
their own.

**Maybe talking
is always good.**

Even when we
disagree.

**Why else
bother?**

Now, go take a
walk in the
woods and if
you meet a
bear, give him
my regards.

M.P. Jones Production

ABOUT THE AUTHOR

M.P. Jones, Jr. is an irreverent humorist who delves deep into absurdity.